COLLECTION *of* POETRY

by Corliss Rush

DORRANCE PUBLISHING CO
EST. 1920
PITTSBURGH, PENNSYLVANIA 15238

Dorrance Publishing Co
585 Alpha Drive
Suite 103
Pittsburgh, PA 15238
Visit our website at *www.dorrancebookstore.com*

ISBN: 979-8-88683-633-2
eISBN: 979-8-88683-634-9

'A Life Journey'

My poetic ways and my life are finally changing.
As we get older our life stories begin calling; trying to set themselves free.

'To be exposed for the world to see'

There are layers upon layers of real-life experiences,
Some are strange but true; when some are told it's hard for people to
believe you.

I've had things to happen that were truly more explainable as if invisible
people were the answer. Where things happen that blow you away.

Do you say is it make believe or is that real; does age change their ways
or make things different? Do your eyes leave you wondering?

Did I see what I thought I saw; was that even possible?
Sometimes you hope it wasn't ever there; sometimes your mind can't
even comprehend it.

As we live and grow, we know that life is stronger than fantasy or fiction.
As you live your experiences builds and builds.

'The more you age the more you can give.'

'The things you have done good will become your shining light, the
wrongs will become your building block.'

I see how getting older is one of God's great blessings.

We become mentors to the younger generation. Our wisdom and knowl-
edge tell us that God is in the thick of things; in every phase of life.

The older I get the more I recognize that Jesus must become our standard.
The one and only true commander.
That everyone young and old should always honor.

I'm so glad I've lived this long;
I believe my life will continue on; or at least for the now.

I haven't been good all my life; and I haven't done all bad;
it takes the both of them to always be had.

But through it all I have been saved by Jesus Christ and his precious
love; also by his precious everlasting grace.

"Nostalgic"

If only time could stand still, and stay a certain way; where things were simple; where things were slow, back in the day. Once upon a time children were kids, they develop slow; stage upon stage brought on the worldly growth.

We would play together and have big fun; there were never any guns. Fights were far and few between, when it was over you shook hands and never held revenge; you fixed the problem right then and now; something that faded like air.

Our families were super special, we loved and respected our mommy and daddy; they become our idols; we could not become grown up too fast. You had your place and you were glad.

Once upon a time you did as you were told, if you went somewhere on your own; and told to be back; once upon a time you honored that, kids will be kids, and people will be people. Once upon a time it seemed to have greater meaning.

The morals seem different back there, respect seem to come from within; you learned it at home; just from being around your brothers and sisters. Fighting each other was strictly forbidden.

I wish that point in time would come back again, where the normal isn't so frightening. Where family ruled, where it was king, where you enjoyed the flow of life; where it was nice and slow and never too fast.

All the family members had their part. That point for time is gone forever, the world didn't change it was the people. The world will never stop spinning.

The people have changed their ways and their hearts; once upon a time morals and families loved that part. Now it's all about injustice and disrespect; we wish things would get better, sooner rather than lately.

It is not the case now days; it will never be that way again; seem like we are headed for destruction. Maybe it's true, the people of the world need a time out for sure.

Something to make them see that this is not the way things were meant to be; killing each other on a daily basis; what is the real reason for all of this tension. The people of the world are so amazing.

They shoot instead of trying to talk things over. Oh, if we could have our once upon a time again, things would be very different, for children, for women, and men. I hope and pray that someday it will come back our way.

When we can show honor, love, and understanding for who so ever is our earthy neighbor. That's my earthly hope for the world today, where all life is precious. Where everyone's heart could be as one. Sharing love like God and his only son, the one and only Jesus Christ.

"An Ode to Love"

Love is such a pretty word, 4 letters is all it consist of. A small word with very big meaning

Love: we all seek it and we all need it for our own gratification.

Its power is a force for good if use for the right intentions. Love: it fit us all, big or small it does not matter, short or tall.

God made us for this holy virtue. To share our life with pure devotion. Love is a heartfelt emotion.

Love: we can't contain the power it has, we must pass it on so it will last. When it is inside of you, you will glow. Happiness and goodness will always show.

Love: is the purest of all emotions, when it is true, it will transform you. You are not the same anymore, your eyes shine, your inside begins to rise.

The main thing about love is you become smitten, then bitter, once love touch you, you are hooked to the bone, love: you want that feeling to forever last.

Love: can take you on the highest high. Make us feel like we are floating in the sky. Love: it's put your heart in a special place and take that very same heart and set it on fire.

The greatest part of love to me is how God gave it to us for free. When God made love I do not think he could have made anything better.

Love: is such a big part of himself, that is the reason we have to share it. He knew what the power of love could do.

That is why it come from your heart shared by two. Who hasn't been touched by this glorious power, your first love will never get old.

The splendor of love goes deep in to the soul. Love was made to be shared by two or more, it all up to you for sure.

Each of us holds the key to unlock love purity. Love is never abusive, love is very holy and love is a part of God great mercy.

Love: it touches our deeper parts and makes us feel like we are 10 feet tall. That feeling is universal. It is inside of us all; whether we are full grown or very small.

Love: is such a beautiful thing, until you feel as if you have wings. Time and distance do not matter. Love: the power is sometimes like cancer.

Love: is a fruit of the spirit and the sweetest fruit there is. Love: there is so much to say about it. It is so grand that the world can't live without it.

The world needs love to share; to touch the heart of women and men, and to make everything become fair. Love is our guiding light.

A light that shone the brightest by day. Love: is always here to stay and love will never go away. That is the best way. If it went away the world could die.

That part of life that deals with sharing I mean. Love: it must be passed on, to women, to children, and men.

From ancient time till now, love will go on and on and love will forever stay strong. If there is one thing the world needed now is love, always in ample supply.

Enough to change the heart of everyone in the world today. Love: that is why God made it to share. Ever since man learned to read and write;

Love has been a part, that special part, that beautiful part to always write about. That expression of the soul that must be told. This is my written version of love.

May it be forever told as it forever unfolds. Love is a mystery in 4 letters. Love: the most compelling word in the entire world, in history and our nation.

I know there is more to say about this wonderful thing called love, I know that it come from above. I know that God is love and love is his biggest part.

Our image of God is our love part. The way God share it is how we should share also. When we love one another, we become God like ourselves.

We unleash invisible power, a power that is good as can be, we give it to other people and help set them free.

Love: is our freedom plus liberty, and our honorable mention. One of God greatest gifts filled with goodness.

Love: was made for the human race. Love is the purest part of God holy grace. Embrace love with all your heart.

Let it become the biggest part of all. I have said a lot up until now. I know there is still more to be said. Love: is never ending and always intending.

Love: is always trying to grow, love is always looking for something to sow. Love wants to stay in touch with the soul of man, it wants to be that power to heal.

To heal all wounds of women and men. Love: it wants to be handed down, love: it wants to wear the golden crown for everyone.

Love: the most beautiful thing shared by human beings. Since I started this mini epic, love is still revealing herself to me even better.

As you let love grow, these are some of the things love will bestow, it will give you humility with tenderness, patience is also there beside forbearance.

Love: it takes those 4 good fruits and make them true.
Love: it put us up close to God and man.

Love: is an active principle when express with the right intention. Love is the choice we have to make and love is the one we should take.

In this fallen world love is the fulfillment of God's law, love: it does no wrong to any neighbor. The biggest part of the human race is to love from a pure heart.

A good conscience and God given faith, love: is a way of thinking that will always lead us to our greatest behavior.

God loves a loving person, one who is gentle and humble and one who is full of compassion.

I will end my words and writing, I am very happy and glad love had its say, but what is best of all, I did it my own special way.

Amen; thank you for these words my Heavenly Father.

How far away only one knows the number of stars? And all their names; man surely can't, not even the angels. Only one possesses the mind-blowing wisdom.

"Jesus Christ, he's unbelievable."

It is fearful to think that the stars are his testament, He places each and every one; gave them their space. Some to be out of most reaches.

"I wonder why God made so many."

To show mankind that you will always be little, to show that he is wisest and above all. All the technology and the world today I can't count the stars anyway.

"God grace must extend out of this world."

Even the stars must bow down and serve him, mankind can live billions of years and never understand what Jesus did, or what he can do.

"How deep and profound his wisdom go."

He shows small and big pieces of what he thinks we should know. It's so mind blowing how he knows the number of stars.
"He even knows the distance they are apart."

He's the only expression that gave them their start; mankind can't even come close to match the stars number. They will never be able to count them.

"Only Jesus, the master mathematician."

He knows how many grains of sand there are; or even better, how many blades of grass there are; there is nothing he does not know.

Numbers are nothing to him and the stars are no exception.

Fearing him we become his children, knowing that he is incomprehensible; he's just amazing and he is all we need.

"There is no need for two."

He's always true; he's the one and only true living God; the only one to know it all; there will never be other.

"A Mind Journey"

My mind, the one I know, loves to keep busy. Activity feels like fog and splendor.

Stagnating will never enter into it. It seems to always seal.

It sits and waits for the smallest inkling that becomes a miracle.

Taking something from nothing and making something is a very, very special thing.

The same way our Heavenly father did for creation. That small kindness is the soil for all creation.

It's a small spark with a precarious birth. It's up to us to make it work.

There are so many choices when that spark exist. You have to make the right discovery.

One that is far filling and one that is very pleasing

I do not fight the whims of intelligence motion; they carry me to exquisite poetry; the kind that seem so rare.

I go deep within to reach the very core. There is a center to deep thinking.

One that's in the middle from start to finish; it's a very rare gem and its golden.

Sometime only death can exterminate it; Oh, who knows if that spark will live or die.

Death could awaken our purest power and the truest.

An everlasting activity, if it's doing nothing but praising Him, that small spark will become a fire.

Shining bright and very pure.

Then we have surely seen the light.

A Note to Myself:

This came to me very spontaneous; it was so mind blowing it took meanings to express my innermost feelings; a no. 1 and a no. 2, they both are trying to convey my message to you.

It never ceases to amaze me how Jesus is always before us; how we can speak and not move our lips; so much of life is forward thinking it will take you back to the source; there you can see the goodness of it; knowing this goodness has to have protection; and wisdom that was without question; what is wonderment to us is how to love; that is why he is the one and only, whether we speak or not, it does not matter, he can hear our thoughts just like we pray sometime so very silently; A hard journey always has our end; it's backward road or path has its beginning; with a one and only true living God; Jesus is our point of origin; think long enough and you will see him, a shining light to all your thought, a true light that never dim or never go out. He is the real one no doubt.

"Another one and done; another space poem"

I have one poem about space already; it seems like the time had come for another, right now for sure.

Space: do you ever think about it?
Was it in the beginning?
Did our Heavenly father invent it?

Space: it's everywhere without being seen. Every story in existence has a part of it.

Space: where is it beginning and its ending? Does it have one; it could be just like Jesus always attending.

Space: Is never full, everything for the world today has its place; in space and is always on display. It takes a lot of space for everything to have their place.

All the stars and all the planets need vast amount of space to keep their orbit. Time and space seem different; on earth; we do not have light years to judge the distance. Things seem to be closer on earth.

We can go around our world; try going around the universe, you'll never make it. I know space can never change; it will always remain the same.

Space: seem like nothing but I know it's something, look at the world and you will never see it. It is very, very invisible.

Space: it has always been in existence; one of God great principles; he has so very many.

To see all of God's creations, to see the order, space: let us see life and death, the change of the seasons, how people think and how they reason.

Space: bring everything to light, it shows the answers for daylight and the night. Space: we are a part of it, it's always trying to be filled but it never will.

There is an essence to space and I believe it's time; where everything for space is a part of. There is a place for space for everyone; everything must live and die as God intended.

Everything that comes to live will always have their space; once their time is here. Space: is such a place, that I wish I could reach out and touch it.

There is nothing physical about it, it's just an invisible dimension, where everything in God's creation fit.

Jesus was the beginning and the end; and space was his best friend. Jesus understands space true meaning.

Even before creation came; the space was needed; so creation could come forth, just the way everything was intended.

Space: is truly a grand enigma, it will never be understood by man, just like our Heavenly Father Jesus. I tried to shed a small piece of light on this thing we call space.

Only Jesus knows the truth, and space will be forever; always to exist. So the next time you look around; up or down, you know that space will be forever around.

In this world or the next; space is on God's side and they will be here forever.

"Jesus Coming"

Jesus came with a plan in mind; to live among us and still be divine. To show the way his Heavenly father is.

The way to live and how to give. Back in the days when Jesus was here the people wanted him to disappear.

They did not believe he was God only son; how could that be and he was only a man. It was love told in the days of old that Jesus was coming.

His coming and his death were ground breaking; no one never did the things he did, he was God in the flesh for the world to see.

Jesus coming was simple as can be; to save sinners and to set us free. God must complete everything he starts.

We started in paradise; that is mankind highest calling; the Eden he made while things were young, we will get back because of his son.

The love Jesus gave is beyond compare; his whole existence is about not quitting.

Jesus coming paved the way for every lasting life his father way. The father and son do everything as one.

Jesus is coming back again, coming to give the world another chance to win.

Winning is for Jesus' second coming.

"A Story of David Shortened"

Saul was the king that God people wanted.

They wanted someone to rule over them like all the others. The Lord heard their cry and he raised up Saul by and by. Saul would rule but it would not last. David was a young shepherd boy who God loved with his whole heart.

God knew that Saul time was drawing near, very soon Saul's life would have to disappear.

God knew David was the true king. One who had the right heart.

While tending the flock God taught him right. Gave him courage to stand very tall; God knew he would need it. He fought and fought the enemies of God.

Just waiting on God and his time to rule it all.

And it came to pass that the Lord sent Samuel to Jesse's house to sacrifice. To Bethlehem he went. Not knowing that David was next to be king; the living God always knows everything.

Inside the house Samuel saw them all. Samuel still did not see David who was the very last.

The Lord sees not as man. God looks at the heart, David heart was the biggest of all.

David was outside keeping the sheep making sure they were safe as God had meant. When David came in they were all surprised, knowing that Samuel had chosen David to be king over all God's people and Israel too.

Now the Philistines' got together to make war with God's people. They did not know about David and how God was with him. The Philistines had a mighty warrior, bigger than all the rest, whose name was Goliath and David put him to the test.

When the men saw Goliath and how big he was, they took off running and were very afraid. All except David. David told the people, let no man's heart fail because of this man. I will fight him in the name of God. I have faith I will win. Even though I am in my youth. The living God will deliver me. He took his staff and five smooth stones; plus faith in God, Goliath fell dead at his feet.

And it came to pass that day, David and Goliath would have their battle and Goliath would lose in a very big way. He looked upon David and knew he had a sure win. He had never met anyone like David with his stones and his sling. David told him: I come in the name of the Lord of hosts. You have defied him and now you will know. He gives me my power and this I know for sure.

Now David put his hand in his bag, took one stone and slung it, the stone struck into his forehead, the battle was over before Goliath hit the ground. When the Philistines saw he was dead, their whole army turn around and fled.

When I read about David life and how he was, I knew he had faith in the living God. There is so much to say about this man of God and of old. He was king for 40 years until he became old. He had battles all his life and God pulled him through as only he could do. David had all it takes to be a great king. He was very valiant with all his men. They respected him one and all. The common people loved him because they knew he was a man of God. He was not perfect but he was selected to rule God people and to make them better. The story of David could fill many books, David was very special and God knew it.

"Not enough love"

There is not enough love in the world today, people have literally thrown it away. Love for life is not precious anymore. Hearts are cold, very cold right now I'm here to say.

When love is by your side your hatred and deception will vanish like the wind blowing clouds; like the sun or rain; love will make everything different, people will take on a whole new meaning.

Doing wrong will leave and righteousness will rule. Love has been taken away for now anyway; in its place badness and decay. Love for your fellow man must take center stage again. The world is so cruel today.

People are wild and are very rare; doing right has taken a wrong turn. Mankind has become low, predators rule the day and innocent people become prey; even children become part of the play.

I wish with all my heart that people would love each other and become more loving. If one Godly wish were granted to me, I would let love go free; to every village and town.

To everywhere and all around; I would let it flow;
In ample supply I would let it go.

To every heart that's alive right now today; I would let love take away the hate that is on display. Love is our guide and to everlasting peace that the whole world seeks. I know love is the answer.

I know it take this earthly career and nip it in the bud. The only truth we can have is love. Love gives us clarity and focus, make our words and life truly count for something.

Being closely aligned to God is our part of God golden rule. The impression God gave will help us live as true sons and daughters of our Heavenly father. Where love come out the heart is the key.

If love is not there your goodness will never appear. We should always know that God is the only one we should ever follow; he never run out of love; you can bet your very last dollar.

"Another Year"

They say another year has come into play, that is what mankind has to say. How do they know that a year has passed; are the days different from the last one?

You had day and night and night and day are always perpetual; they will never go away; when did out with the old and in with the new become your

View; how does one year make another one new. Mankind is the master deliverer of time; take it and twist it up.

He takes years, days, hours, and minutes, making them to become special units; 24 hours equals one day; seven days make a week, 365 is the no. of days

To complete a year. There have been so many years of old; they were once called ancient. Time always make time old.

That is why 2019 is not new; time will stay perpetual; all you have to do is see it. It's normal for the world to think this way is what I say.

Time isn't old and it's never new, I guess that is what I'm trying to tell you; the one year is gone and another is here.

Another way the world thinks man is the ruler of this world and his methods are very wrong. Say something enough and you start believing it.

The truth is clear; time can't be broken up, it's eternally near. That part of time does not belong to man's mind, it's outside his thinking. Man lives by the changes he's made.

In the early days, time was stable, you had day and night, hot and cold, the rain or shine. We are the bigger parts of the rhythm of life.

Life was simple and nature was the show; it worked out and here we are; to older time to now.

Still talking about a new year as all the supposedly one is gone. I think a different way and I'm glad I do.

I hope what I say will do you good as you go on your way. I hope I've shared a small piece of light on a tradition that is not right.

Be careful of the ways of man; asking is his only true way; there is no new year that will ever belong to you; all of time is His.

God given; given to us by God and his one and only son; Jesus Christ.

"The Idea"

One idea is all I needed to bring something to people that they can read. Poems is what I do, I do them with the up most flavor.

Hoping your taste buds will always savor, trying to make sure they are made to order. I want what I have to say to come alive in every way.

Something that is good and true that you always say to you. One idea was the starting point for everything that's here. One idea made it all appear.

Ideas can become very powerful weapons, and it turn men into modern human beings. Ideas are invisible things that float through your

Mind like they have wings. They take the cause and add the effect to it, they make that clear become dear and they are always near.

The profound things of the world today started with basic ideas alone the way. The idea from horse and buggy lead the way to our car; the car

Was much better than the horse and buggy; plus we did not have too ride in bad weather. The idea of irrigation lead to more crops for our nation.

Small wooden boats became giants made of steel; ideas are the start of all the inventions. All the things we see today some one idea led the way.

I am glad I see how good certain ideas can be.
The right ideas will always set us free.

The poems I've written have turned to stories, not epics but short and very pleasant. They have a certain way all their own. Spoken from a poet point of view

Of course, join together to create something similar. Their flavor is very tasteful and never bitter. I see a style and flair all their own. They have a simple

Tread, make them belong to my own unique form. I had this feeling a long time ago that my poems could become a story. Sure enough, that notion was true and now I bring stories to you.

I've always known that 2 is better than one when they agree, they become very strong. I read and reread my work all the time. It feels like a live body.

Getting stronger every day and every hour, feel like my poems are evolving. I can see life in my work and a power coming forth. When you read these

Words all you can feel is my heart and my true worth. My whole life is for what I write, my words are an open book. The way my mind is my

Writing will lead the way. I'm always a work in progress always seeking the truth. Trying to get closer to the living God.

I understand now he rule my heart, I understand so much now, he's the biggest part of all. Of everything that's here; he put everything together.

Time to him is really nothing. The poems I have new or old can't stop the stories that must be told. Time is really nothing, when you take time to put your

Thoughts and all your passion on the lowly piece of humble writing paper.

"Old Man Time"

As old man time has its way; you will age just like night and day; you can't outdo old man time. No matter how you live it will beat you.

There is a good virtue in being older; the best one is you have lived longer. Getting older let you see that sooner or lately death will come for you.

As older men we are blessed to go through stages that lead to rest; the kind of rest that mellow you out; to know you have done a few things right.

Being young is a beautiful time; you have energy and your mind is like a grape vine. Things are plucked from you; things are put back into you also.

Old man time is the same to us all; as long as you have it; having it will take the young away; the middle age to; having it will lead to gray hairs for me and you.

I wouldn't trade my age I have now; I am very glad to have lived this far; I hope old man time will give me grace; time enough to mend my ways.

Time enough to love the Lord; time enough to keep me small. I'm glad God made old man time and I have my portion.

We never know what time has in store, we have to do our best and make it work for us, old man time is good as can be.

Use it wisely and then you will know how good you can really be, old age is not for one and all; for some people the chance never comes at all.

Some die younger before their life has even started; be thankful if your years are long; God is the one who give old age its song.

My old age is full of delight filled with many days and of nights.

"The Old Lady"

This has been on my mind all day long and I knew if I didn't write this, it would never leave my mind alone.

Long ago while I was walking in a town called Columbus, I looked up ahead and my eyes saw a treat, a little old lady waiting just

For me. It seemed to me that day that I was meant to help her on her way. As I got near, things became very clear.

I could see that she needed help crossing the street; she was standing and waiting for someone to help her, and it was me.

People were passing her by as if they didn't care. Some people stood right by her side; they didn't take a small piece of time to sacrifice.

They were too full of their own selfish pride, when I got to her spot she was still standing there.

Still waiting to cross that street. I went across to the other side and told her I would help her if she didn't mind.

While I spoke those words to her, her spirit became glad. I took her hand and we cross over once again.

She went into a neighborhood store; she had an angelic glow; I was waiting and soon she was ready to go.

We went back across the street; I had to make her day become totally complete. When she began to go home; this is what

She said to me: God must have sent you this day and also sent you my way. I will never forget that special day when

I helped the little old lady that I looked upon from far away.

"A Story about Jesus"

I want to write about Jesus; the last part of his life on earth. It was not good and not very nice at all.

What he went through and how he suffered; only he could do. He had a special job and he had to see it through.

The priests and scribes were Jews too; they could not understand how Jesus could be God and man and still maintain

When they got Jesus it was night; they had to wait for first light before they could convince him to keep it right.

Pontius Pilate had Jesus case at first light, he was always up before dawn to make sure his day started out right.

He had a lot to do each day; the power he had made him have his way.

Pilate was the one who arrested Jesus; he called him a trouble-maker; he did not know who Jesus was; he did not know that Jesus was God son.

When Jesus stood before this man; Pilate asked what he had done; while walking this land. No one had a direct answer, it all came from not understanding.

The people said: if he were not a criminal, we would not have brought him to you.

Pilate had killed a lot of Jews but something about Jesus made him want to change the rules.

He was not like other prisoners Pilate had seen; he was humble; very meek and subdued in his speech, the people said we have no power to execute!

Sometimes they stoned or strangled without a true account; especially if you were a gentile; you had very few rights.

The evil leaders of that day wanted Jesus crucified without delay. Crucifixion was capital punishment in that day.

Very cruel and a very painful; you could be crucified on a standing tree near the place of your crime or at a crossroad.

You would be hung from a tree with nails in your hand and feet. Death was slow but it came for sure.

The Jews knew from scripture that anyone hanged on a tree was cursed; they did not want to believe because they had seen Jesus at his best.

Pilate asked Jesus to state his defense; Jesus did not answer; he knew that all was meant.

Pilot asked Jesus: are you the king of the Jews? The Jews wanted him to be a king; it was hard for them to see it was not his thing.

Pilate said I find no wrong in this man; they said Jesus had brought disruption for the land.

Jesus said he and God are the same; all the people knew was that Jesus was just a man.

Pilate gave in and sent Jesus on; to Herod who did not care anyway.

While they went to see Herod Pilate got to work. Hearing cases that put two men to their death. A third case came and Barabbas was his name.

He had committed murder and was a popular freedom fighter, he was well liked by the people and they wanted him to keep on living.

They have rules that were not fair and this was one the people put up in the air; chosen by the people by acclamation.

Meanwhile; Jesus was before Herod; he was superstitious and he had a lot of greed. He killed John the Baptist just because he could.

He showed pleasure at the opportunity to talk to Jesus; plus he wanted to see a miracle. The prosecution hurled charges; Jesus did not even answer.

Herod took Jesus as a joke; they put him in a gorgeous robe; made fun of him truth be told.
Herod tried of this and sent him back to Pilate; Pilate was the one who pronounce his end.

Herod did not find reason to kill Jesus and Pilate felt the same way; things had to be in order to stay true.

Pilot wanted to have Jesus beaten, a lesson for the people to see and then set him free.

Shall I release to you the king of the Jews; the people wanted Barabbas set free; the people said crucify him, he needed to be dead.

Pilot knew there was nothing he could do; as a first step he ordered Jesus to be a scourge; to be beaten very bad; they wanted Jesus to snap or even to go mad.

This was the preliminary to crucifixion; Pilate was trying to get by trying not to murder Jesus; he could not find a reason why; all he heard was the people evil cry.

Syrian soldiers took Jesus away; for interrogation is what they said. Jesus was stretched with hands over his head; a clerk took down everything that was said; either screams or confessions.

He was led to a courtyard where a whipping pillar-waist high, was between him for washing the blood away; they had already use them on the two thieves that day.

Now they stripped Jesus naked; beat him over the pillar; made him so his back, buttocks, and his legs were exposed.

Two big slaves stood nearby ready to do the whipping; each picked up a whip of three leather thongs; the slaves were very strong.

They brought down their whips with all their might; the whips had lumps of bones to really bring the pain out.

They hit Jesus very hard; the whips cut through the skin, nerves, and muscles; this had to be very, very painful.

They lashed his shoulders and spinal cord; his buttocks and thighs; they whip his chest and ribs, a flogging like this could some time kill.

They had to leave enough strength to carry the cross beams to the site; Jesus did not even cry out.

With superhuman power he endured it all; with great courage he stood very tall.

When the whipping stopped, he was unburdened; stood in his own blood; shivering from shock; cut and bruised from shoulder to his calves; soon it would be his last time on the earth.

They put a cloak on him to protect his nakedness; and the horror was just beginning.

They fashioned a garland of thorns, shaped like a crown; Jesus had to wear it without a frown.

The thorns made blood trickled from his temples; to Jesus it was all very simple; to mock the son of man.

All their hatred of the Jews erupted as they seized the thorns and hit him on the head; driving the thorns deeper into his head.

The soldiers came in and kneeled; to spit and slap his face; he took it all and never said a word.

Out of the shadows, slowly and painfully he came; wearing a purple robe and his crown of thorns.

His face marked by agony; his robe was soaked in blood; this was meant and it had to be told.

Behold the man; Pilate cried; then a noise rose up from the crowd. They talked very evil; and were very loud.

Crucify, crucify him was what they said, they really wanted him dead.

Pilate brings Jesus in again; ask him where he come from; Jesus said nothing again.

Will you speak to me he says; Jesus said inside himself; I am ready to be on my way.

Pilate told the people he is not responsible for the death of this innocent man; it is your doing; it is not in my hands.

On the cross he will go; for the end you shall know.

On this Friday, April 7 A.D. 30; the sun was already strong; a young smart Centurion was to supervise Jesus execution.

The slaves came first, caring ladders, rope, four nails, and hammers.

The logs were about 6 foot long and lay ready for the cross beams; you had to carry your own.

Jesus came into the sunlight, wearing his own clothes; and the thorns were his own.

Across his shoulders lay a heavy beam; it weighed down his body. He was weak from loss of blood, lack of sleep and food; after a few feet he staggered and fell to the ground.

His father in Heaven knew he needed help; an African name Simon gave him a hand. He had two sons; they all believed in Jesus and on this day they won.

Relieved of his burden Jesus walked on. The women followed every step of the way. Mary was bravely determined to stay.

The crowd moved toward the gate of the city; where the ground began to rise to a hill overlooking Jerusalem.

A rocky outcrop was waiting there; the place of the Skull. It was dominated by tree trunks, erected for crucifixions.

Used again and again for all of its history.

One pleasant feature was found; a beautiful garden was around it belonged to Joseph of Arimathaea; a very good Christian man.

The Centurion made a brief inspection and found the site all right. Jesus was put in the middle of both convicts.

Four executioners put hand on Jesus and stripped him bare; a man was crucified naked weather a gentile or Jew.

They threw Jesus to the ground; not caring that his back was torn and tender; and his head had a circle of thorns; only worn by one.

Two soldiers held out his arms; a third put the cross beam under them, the fourth pressed hard at his knees.

A long hammer and nails were used; one held his arm and put the nail above his palm.

With a sharp blow the nail went through his hand into the cross beam; the pain he felt was very intense.

He did not scream out but cried out Abba Father. Each blow increased the pain: Jesus prayed to his father, forgive them; they know not what they do.

That is why I came to see them through.

When they finished nailing him to the cross, one of them climbed the ladder, others lifted the beam with Jesus on it.

This was when the pain was at its worst. They crossed his legs, put the feet against the tree, put nails into each, the nails had to stay in place.

While on the cross the flies and stinging insects began to crawl. The blood flowed from his hands and feet.

He could barely move or get his breath; the more he breathed, the more he bled. The agony was taking its toll, cramps shooting through his arms and legs.

The wounds from the whipping, the thorns, the nail, the pitiless sun, and his thirst; he was already in shock.

Jesus endured it all because he was called. His father was there but he still had to bear it all.

They hurled insults at Jesus as he hung on the cross, you saved others but you can't save yourself, come down and we will believe; they were all fools.

The thieves, suffering the same; said to Jesus: if you are the Christ save yourself and us; one said we did the crimes, this man has done nothing wrong.

One asked Jesus to remember him when you come into your kingdom. Jesus told him you will be with me in paradise.

By now, after almost 3 hours, the torture had worked its magic on Jesus' body. He looked very bad indeed.

His physical beauty and his goodness were gone, he was contorted, disfigured, despicable, blood dripped from his hands and feet.

Lips and face and he had sun blisters, plus insect bites, you could not tell if it were Jesus anymore.

He was in for a bad way and he still saved the day; plus his bones stuck out from his flesh.

At noon darkness covered the land, not an eclipse, this was God's doing. The strange loss of light gave people something to be scared about. There was no sound all around.

Before the darkness came, Jesus seemed envelope by evil; his struggles were fearful. There was pain, he was taking the sins of the world and a great darkness had his soul.

He had never known darkness like this before, his light was the brightest like none before.

An invisible weight bore down on his soul, the weight of the world. This was no joyous martyr's death.

Jesus sorrow was beyond imagination his grief untold; he was doing his father work, as only he could do.

After 3 hours of darkness, Jesus gave a terrible cry; he said my God, my God, why have you forsaken me.

He said I thirst and they gave him wine and vinegar not water. Suddenly Jesus gave another cry; and he said in a tone of triumph, father into your hands I commit my spirit, gently he bowed his head with it crown of thorns.

A second later he was still and gone.

It came down to Jesus being the good shepherd, no one, take my life from me, I lay it down myself. I have authority to lay it down and to take it again.

Jesus is the one and there is no other; the son of the living God.

"Oasia"

It's a place in time we can't see; we have to wait for it; to come near,
Then it becomes clear.

An Oasia is a blessing that pushes you farther; it's a place to rest. To analyze. To see if you can make it.

We all need an Oasia to come. When our struggles are few and the things we are doing become true.

We are going to get lost and lose our way some time.

Maybe not that lost that we can't find our mind.

We must think of our own Oasia. The one we have inside; where God reside.

The one that does not deal with pride.

Most of the Oasias are in faraway places.
To me that seem absurd.

In the real world where we live; most of us haven't been in a desert place;
Miles and miles from saving grace.

When an Oasia is near, there's where your help lies. It has everything you need to survive.

When I was young, I didn't believe Oasia existed. Time always brings about a change;
And my Oasia was to advance.

I know now that life can be a desert place; where nothing easy come your way.

Sometime we feel like giving up; when all we need is a little luck.

Their out of the blue an Oasia will appear, you can't believe it.

It feels like a second chance; which we all need in this land.

A chance to right the wrongs we have done.
To make us to stay on the straight and narrow;
To always give thanks to our Heavenly father.

To always know you are better when you can see your own Oasia.

Let your Oasia be your way station for life; use it and use it wisely; and stay out of desert places.

'Oasia'

"The Ending and the Beginning"

I have heard that saying a lot of my life, the ending is better than the beginning and I wondered why?

It takes a beginning to make an ending; you can't have one without the other. When something start and it's good, you want it to last the way it should.

When something starts the ending is usually not in sight, it is waiting for the beginning to get there, hoping that the beginning is right.

The only way you get from one to the other, you must invest your time to make each better. I know that when something starts, it is not over.

Nothing can end unless it begins. I think about those things and I can see how both must surely be. We start out with our best intention.

Hoping our ending will have true meaning. Alone the way unseen things will happen; they are waiting to come our way.

Out of the blue they change the beginning, what you thought was right was out of sight and you wanted the end to come. When your beginning is wrong and you finally see, time will make everything as it should be.

I know this without a doubt that the ending is better sometimes than you thought. It takes life to see how this can be.

In the beginning, things start off small, it takes human nature to make us fall, fall for a sense that we see the way.

How one good thing leads to another; how they both come together to help our spirit grow; most of the time when the ending comes, you're not the same anymore.

The ending is stronger than the beginning because you have made it through. The beginning is gone in your life and is moving on where you belong.

"It takes different people to make the world go around"

It takes different people to make the world go around.

Some can do this and some can do that.

Whatever you do belong to you.

People can't make the world spin.

It's a saying said by men.

It would be a shame if we were all the same.

Thinking alike, speaking alike and having the same motive.

It takes variety to fuel society.

Different ideas to appeal to the masses.

It has taken a lot of thinking from different people to achieve what we have today.

One person or one culture will never be enough.

Certain groups of people do what they do the best.

Where they live is for them to give.

The earth was made to be shared by all the races.

The spice of life is all about diversity.

All the resources that are here today;

People everywhere are there for the way.

Goods are shared from all over the world.

Coming from here coming from far away;

We all share God glorious bounty.

Different people and faraway places.

All come together to save the races.

We are all one in God's eyes.

Always inseparable; we are all universally connected.

"The Cross of Christ"

The cross of Christ, what a wonderful act it was, that one act was all it took to save the whole world and more.

It was an event that was planned from the beginning of time, God knew man would not keep his plan.

With love and grace the cross was bound, God made man in such a way that he was to live, still alive forever and a day.

One wrong act was all it took to plunge mankind into the abyss, he could not right the wrong he had done.

The only way to right the wrong was the coming of Christ, God only son. The cross was all about love and to help us grow.

God truly loves us so; a love we can't really know; the cross of Christ represented this, because Christ said so.

The cross of Christ was a onetime thing, come from God; the one and only holy being. The only one who could right the wrong of sinful man.

In the beginning, he made us to live forever. He made us, man and woman, to always stay together.

To be in control and love one another, Jesus and the cross will take us back. It is not hard, all we have to do is believe that.

The cross make us see God like never before, the way he suffered, and how they beat him so, all because he love us so.

Now Christ and the cross has set us free; to live for eternity, in the most wonderful place there can be; Heaven, don't you agree.

There is so much I could say about the cross of Jesus, how it made my day. I know the cross show us love; the love that came down from above.

He died and rose again; the only one to take away sins. Made a way for us to live forever.

The cross and Jesus is our example; and grace is here forever. The cross of Christ, there is nothing better.

"Gladiators — Then and Now"

Long ago in the ancient days of Rome; the Roman Empire had an arena called the Colosseum where blood sport was learned then born.

The Colosseum was big and held lots of people, 50,000 or more could be in attendance; dignitaries and common people; mostly farmers.

They would come to see the Roman gladiators; a blood sport it became in the arena. Men fighting each other to the death. One was going to die was their true test.

I'm not sure women face this ordeal but I'm pretty sure that they did; life back then was very hard and very, very cruel.

All the people who live back then would cheer and shout for their gladiator to win, not by knockout or a serious blow;

But by death or his head taken off by a sword; the arena would explode and everyone wanted more. To make matter worse they added wild animals.

Lions and tigers to devour all mutilated corpses.

The gladiators who won their fight became mighty men in their sight, almost like a folk hero. Fast forward from then until now blood sport still has center stage. People will come from everywhere:

To modern arena to see men and women fight, not to the death like back then but by a knockout punch or submission.

Like then as in the now our modern-day gladiator most still always win. If they are evenly matched, they will end up fighting again; to determine the true winner.

Even now death is there; bullfighting and race car driving just to name a few. The right blow could send you down below. Where you will never rise again.

A lot of time the blood sport itself will win. Why do people love this so? Do they enjoy seeing blood and gore; does seeing someone hurt excite their senses?

Is there an innate sensation that people enjoy seeing other people being hurt and being beaten senseless, or is blood the real factor?

Back in ancient Rome blood sport was king and gladiators were considered the real men; when it came time to fight and kill, the arena was always filled.

People waiting to see this grandiose thing. The victor stood tall and true. Empathy and compassion could never be in you. Gladiators had the man image.

Their pride and ego had to be the highest, they love the crowd and all the cheering. In this day and time, the same is true.

You always want to be the winner and never be the loser. I must admit a substantial fact that competition will drive you; we always want to end up on top.

"Especially for Life-or-Death Situations."

Blood sports will always bring out your very best, for arenas all across the world and filled with cheering people; you want to win at any cost.

You want it to stand tall and you want the crown of never losing, we never get tired of always winning. This thrill that blood sport gives us are our sinful nature.

Satan will always give. Seeing another down and out and dead, lying on their back gives people a certain kind of power and flavor; a power and flavor that come from a hunting another person. The same way Cain did Abel.

It's here to stay that gladiator thinking; we know that being competitive is always contemporary and contribute to mankind way of life.

It's a very big part of human nature. I knew that very high status came with winning back then; you had a better life and special benefit were added to it.

The loser was always finished. He was frowned upon. He went back to the dust from the ground where he came from.

He would have no chance of being a people champion, you could even become a free man. Sometime back there, you belong to the rich and famous.

Being a good gladiator was your way to get from downunder A way to a good life as long as you survive. When you lost your life it become very unstable.

You became like a grain of sand; very small for the eyes of your fellow man; gladiators were considered mighty, mighty men.

"The Night Bird"

The last night before I tried to sleep, I heard a bird singing a very sweet melody. I call him the night bird. Seem like he was outside my window.

I still heard the trains and planes, thence they were gone his singing was strong and very good to me. I focus on it without even trying.

I did not know that birds would sing in darkness, this one did, and he sang for hours. I said to myself, what is he singing for?

Does he have a mate somewhere or is he singing just for me? Could be. Inspiration is always free; I knew it right away.

I got up when the daylight came and his singing had filled my soul all night long. I got up and got my pen and paper and this poem came out.

The singing inspired my mind and poetry came to my hand. I'm so glad he sang to me. He seemed to know that I needed it. I love the small points life has to offer, joy and peace will always follow the night bird, thank you so much. Another thing that is needed.

From the day we are born aging is upon you. And you really can't win; aging has already won. Every day you live aging is beside you. It's in our genes.

Aging very slow is the way I will go. I will not live too fast like I'm in a race; knowing I can't win.

I will not live too slow where life pass me up and I become a no-show. Moderation is the key; to aging gracefully.

It been my mantra most of my days, aging gracefully slows the whole aging process down;

It gives you time to consider what is best for you; to make things in your life more sure.

Living life on the fast-track produces nothing but setbacks, plus your body stays full of stress.

Your heart labors, it starts to work harder, and the aging process really suffers; you look old before

Your time, sickness plays havoc with your health; disharmony is at its best. You do not heal as easily; nothing is like before. You look in the mirror and say to yourself; this isn't me; 20 or 30 years of age has found me. Now it's too late, there is no way I can ever reverse it.

Do something about it before it come to you. Start thinking now about moderation; and the

Role it will play. Start moderating the things you do; from the food you eat; to the right amount of sleep, to exercise to being outside.

Don't drink too much and do not smoke at all; let gratefulness also be a part; do things in a God life

Way. I practice it and now I am 70; I still have a piece of aging to go; doing it nice and slow.

How you think and act is also very important, being positive puts brakes on aging.

When you are happy and content your body knows this is the way life was meant.

Aging gracefully, I wish everyone would try it. To see for yourself how it benefits you.

We know every day that we live the aging process will never stand still, having the right mind

Set is so very vital. It set the stage for gracefulness, in between fast and slow, it is the only way to go. To make your life become a glow.

"The Bible"

I have read numerous book and the written word all my life. I have been
on a quest of sorts; seeking truth and trying to fine it all my life.

The Bible is God word and not man; it is the book that will always
stand. It's a book that has many parts. 66 small books complete it all.

It seems like it was waiting for us to come; for you to read God words
he gave to man. It took over a 1000 years for the Bible to be as

It should; a book above all books, one that only God could produce.
The Bible came to this world so that God word could be heard.

He wanted us to see how his word set us free. The Bible is the truth,
man's ideas will hurt you. From the start of everything there is.

The Bible tells all of everything that is real, we learn about God and
his son; we learn the trueness of everything he has done.

We truly know what is right and wrong. The old is the start and the
new is the ending.

They are a testament of God true Glory. From Genesis to Revelation
the Bible tell it holy story; it's like our road map for life.

It's the only book that take us to paradise, it's the only book that explain
Jesus Christ. The only book that leads to eternal life.

The Bible is packed with plenty of God words, and so many verses; over 53 thousand full of purpose. The King James version has almost a million words.

There is only so much God can say, it up to us to seek the rest. The Bible tells how life began; the start of woman and man. The start of everything we see.

The Bible tells us he is the true creator; it leads the way to true happiness. All the good in the world today come from the Bible and what God had to say.

Contentment and generosity, physical health and resilience, forgiveness too, the Bible will lead us to love. The Bible let us know we have something to live for. That his word is a steppingstone; that we have a place that is our home. The Bible let us know that Jesus loves us so.

That he is the way, the truth and the life. No other book even comes close. The Bible let us know that Earth and Heaven belong to God.

The whole universe included. The Bible tell God story; the only book that has no error. Everything in it is the truth.

God can't lie, it's not in him to do; the Bible is God and all his ways; I am so glad I believe every word it says.

I will believe as long as I live; to me all the Bible does is give, give, and give.

"Cancer — The Demon"

I may have written something already about that deadly enemy. Cancer: there are so many forms, enough to cover everyone.

As I write today, I myself have passed the test, as deadly as it is, it's very deadly. It gets inside of us with ease.

The world says I know not how or why it come. When I say I passed the test, it tried to take me; I fought with all my might.

I got an operation and took radiation treatment too, I am still amazed I am still living today. When doctors tell you that you have it,

It shocks your whole soul, like a shot to your heart; where it leaves a big hole. You will never forget being told you have cancer.

In the beginning, death stays on your mind, wondering if your time is up or do I move on?

Even with the best treatment there is no sure way to say you have won. With me, the afterthoughts are clear:

Am I a real survivor, or is it waiting to take me? I have learned not to stress, to live with my true results.

If cancer takes a hole, then you are through, it acts as the death demon, you are very blessed to get past it.

Thousands die every year, I wonder how I missed it: we all have an appointed time and you will live until it comes.

All sickness does not lead to death, to have my days and nights is so special. The bottom line is upon me now.

I had cancer, and so far I have beat it, was it a fight I was supposed to win? Did I fight it in time?

Did the steps I took stop it, life, cancer, seems like it did; I stop its starting point, it was out before it could go any farther.

I thank Jesus Christ for helping me, the blood test was key, it came from the inside so they could see.

That one step saved me and now I'm here, writing about cancer, our deadly enemy. I know there are other people who understand what I say:

There is truly a cancer community all over this world, some beat it but so many are dead, from cancer.

I write this to unknown faces, you can read this one day soon, knowing you are not alone; just like me

The survivors are a special breed, to have beat that demon. I feel your thoughts and stress; you and me have passed the test.

We are very, very, blessed. We are not going anywhere until we are ready.

"Mass Killings"

Mass killings, why are they so prevalent today? It is something that comes from the world but needs to go away. How did it start anyway?

Babies are key and their parents too. When babies are born, they cannot be prejudiced at all, their behaviors are not biased. All they do is be babies.

They will play and no skin color will ever matter or get in the way. Along the way to being grown, something happens. Someone puts deviant ways and bad thinking inside their mind and heart.

So many were forced into hatred and very bad things, and to hate people of color, which is so unnecessary and such a bad notion.

How we are raised is so important to our days and life. What you teach your kids will sometimes stay. When they are small and teachable, put love and respect into them.

Don't say our race is better than the other, don't teach them hate; tell them we are all the same and skin color does not make a man or woman.

The parents must change their thinking and stay away from teaching hatred. It's a shame how a person and a gun can take so much life away without any concern.

The motives, do they have one? They seem to be psychopaths waiting for their time to shine. To see how many they can kill, more than the next man ever will.

Kids are fair game now, age does not matter, it's just so bad when people do mass killings and shootings. I wish it would go away forever and a day.

The families that have to bear this, how sad it makes them; we never know where death may be, and now mass killings are leading the way.

Society will never stop it. It must come from the inside of a person, especially his heart and also from their parents, grandmothers, and grandfathers, aunts and uncles are always included.

Be careful how you raise your kids, teach them love and respect and always take hatred out of the way.

"The pen is my weapon of choice"

The pen is my weapon of choice; instead of having a gun or a knife; a pen is much more humbling. In the wrong hands, the gun and knife will become very deadly and nothing but a vice.

They give society a false sense of power. Pulling a trigger is an easy form of killing; it's very destructive when it enters a human body; a bullet. A knife is deadly also.

Forcing itself into our flesh; there are so many ways how we can kill or hurt another person; the pen is my weapon of choice. "It has power also." Power to make us wise.

A power to learn the truth, a power to expand your mind. It's something to see you through. "A pen in the right hand will enhance human beings." There is a power to soothe our souls; the pen deals with words.

Believable when you read them from the right writer; they let truths be told. Words are powerful indeed; they must convey the right knowledge and wisdom to completely please.

The pen can also do harm; as well as good. So much of what is written is pure falsehood and make believe.

Outright lies and very deceitful; written so mankind can live in darkness and not into the lightness. The pen is held by the heart and mind just like all other weapons.

The pen must seek the best to write. It must try to write what is right.
He must study with all his might; to make sure: that what he writes will
help someone.

And keep them in the light. I saw the pen as my weapon of choice; from
long ago. All through the years it has helped me grow, to be the person
I am today. To always keep seeking.

To keep trying; to keep my pen always pleasing, always poetical, I try
to help another human being; with the things I write and say; right now
today with truthfulness.

It's the only way; why should my words be deadly bullets or daggers,
something that is so bad that it kills you instantly; I do not want my
weapon; the pen; to never

Hurt you, no, not ever, and when you look at them and they belittle
you; my pen must have power; very positive. The only kind that
matters. Something to help heal and to mend

You. To put you back together to spread the loving power. The pen is
my weapon of choice; I am using it every day; trying to keep the dark-
ness away; all with good word play.

"A Small Masterpiece"

I finally found a good writing pen it felt good in my hand like they were best friends; when it came my way, I was glad to say that I am using pens again.

I know we will have good things to say, I love pens and pencils for what they do. They bring out my best. Without them, poetry would not come your way.

Writers need a way and a mean to express their true feelings. A pen or pencil in my hand is a positive thing. It makes life good for men, women, and children.

One writing form does not fit all, the pen or pencil make it fair for the whole world to share. The pen and pencil are simple things, put paper in the mix and they

Become our instruments, a key to our soul which always seek to unfold; to let that creative part always be bold; to let our passions have their wings

To fly away to seek the unseen. One more thing I must say; my pen or pencil plus paper are very motivational, they open up my creativity, they put words

On the printed page. They let thoughts have their way, they help the world be a better place; they give peace to the human race

Having a pen or pencil and not using them brings injustice for you and me; they finish what our mind and heart and the end is always better than beginning.

"The Evil Men Do"

The things men will do some time seem to be untrue and very bad indeed, you wonder how they can do it, are they that evil.

Men murder, they rape, they shoot and do anything they can to another person; even poison. Men will find a way to kill.

Some turn themselves into serial killers; if they get away once they won't stop. Their souls dark and hooked on evil.

Evil is what they are about; how can a person take a life and not think twice, how can they have no feeling when you see a person die right in front of you.

How can you go on and on seeing people die. The thing a man will do has no limit. Little children are sometime their victim.

Are these men devil possess, were they born this way, were they abuse and never had love the way they should.

Did their parents hurt them so, did love leave their heart.? Bad circumstances and bad people are not made for the human race. Being unloved brings about bad outcomes.

I watch programs and I read also and I see all the bad that men do; it started long ago and it will never go away.

Do they know anything about karma or do they care? They will kill until they're caught or die. I still can't understand how they do it.

It seems so cold and not normal at all, killing and taking a life; how do
you live with what you have done do your head block it out.

Do you feel you are right? Your conscience is very dark; there is very
little light anywhere. Inside.

The thing men do seem so untrue, there must be a reason why, to them
anyway. Something motivates them something dark and very evil.

We may never understand why they do it, why they kill their fellow
men, women, and children.

How can you show no love at all; do horrible things like it nothing at
all. I thank Jesus I am not that way.

I can't believe what they will do or what they will say; life is not precious
to them; jail or a bad end is waiting.

Wow; the evil that men will do is truly unbelievably; their hearts are
really corrupt.

"The Poet's Eyes"

The poet's eyes; Oh, how far they see. They take the simple things that all around, give them new meaning, make them profound.

Thoughts become images, they become life itself. They seize the mind and soul. Give you something that your spirit can hold.

Make your spirit soar like the wind; the poet's eyes make you see that this world is not what it should be.

They can make any time or any day; any part of a year; they can make it become good and very dear.

They have a way with their words. Sometime and they are few, but they make everything new.

They say things ordinary writers can't say. They can take a few words and convey a whole story.

Feelings and emotions; just like the oceans: they take you to the heart of what they see. They show us life true essence.

Some of the things a poet say will truly take you away. Their eyes have a special sight. They write what they see whether wrong or right.

They make us feel small sometimes, especially when they write about the simple life: how joy is there all around.

How tragedy is in there also to be found. They call it as they see it, but for a special way.

The poet eyes see from his spirit, from the big to the small, the poets' eyes are never satisfied.

So until this world and the people in it find true peace, the poet's eyes will keep on trying to explain it.

"Butterflies Retreat"

My week is coming to an end
I did a little something and I am very please.
Tomorrow I will edit and rewrite my work;
I love this part best of all.
To get all the mistakes out.
To do away and make things straight.
The pureness will come forth.
My words speak for myself::

I came outside
I walked around
there I found a spot
Butterflies were there to be found
I look at a small spot of ground
everywhere they were
flying to and fro
going from flower to flower
eating their nectar
It seem like their heaven
I look and watched their behavior
some came close
then they were gone
I look some more
to my surprise
small bees were there
Also.

www.ingramcontent.com/pod-product-compliance
Lightning Source LLC
Chambersburg PA
CBHW061359140726
47997CB00003B/1274